HABIT POWER

POWERFUL HABITS TO OVERCOME PROCRASTINATION

CHARLIE HARPER

CONTENTS

Introduction	v
1. What is a Habit?	1
2. Habits and Goals	7
3. How to Break Bad Habits	11
4. Habit Forming 101	21
5. Effective Time Management	28
6. Tips To Help Cope With Bad Habits	34
7. Tips for Procrastination	40
Afterword	47

INTRODUCTION

Habits are something that people pick up in their lives. There are many habits out there. They can be good or bad, beneficial or harmful, and they are a part of a person's daily life. They are needed in order to do things in life, and a simple habit can actually help you become a better person.

There are a lot of habits out there that we all develop. The problem is, some habits are better than others. It's important to look at each of the habits that you have and determine for yourself what you think of them. It's also important to kick those bad habits to the curb, for they can be a problem for you.

But what if you don't know about these habits? What if you have something that others comment upon and say is not good. The problem is, many don't' know how to control those habits, and they can take over the lives of people. Some people call these habits addictions, but habits can be something small that impacts one's life in a good or bad way. The bad habits are the worst, and people need to learn how to get rid of them.

But the question is how?

The first thing to learn is the importance of habits. Habits are something that a person takes up, and it's something that they themselves do. Whether conscious of it or not, habits are something that a person controls. You can control your habits, you just need to learn the best ways to do so. This book is the answer to helping you with your habits, for it will give you some vital information on how to control habits along with the power of habits and how they are formed.

In this book, you'll not only learn about what a habit can do to you, you can also learn how to change a habit or even get rid of it. So you can start changing that habit of being late to work, you just have to read this book and learn about the power of habits and how to control them. You can control your life and your habits, and it's as simple as starting with this book.

You'll even get some cool exercises and tips on where to start with controlling your habits. Habits are important to work on, and if you don't take care of them and get rid of the bad ones, you're going to continue to have a rough time. And you don't' want to live a rough life right? Well the best answer to fixing that problem is to start on your journey to a better life full of good habits and getting rid of the bad ones. Because you can do it, you just need some help.

Habits can be a problem, especially when they stick around and become troublesome for most people. But don't worry, you can control it. You'll be able to do so with this helpful book. This will be the start of your ability to see the power of a habit and what it can do if you keep it around, along with ways to help you change your own habits so they can become something better than anything you've ever expected before.

All people can control their destinies and their

outcomes. Controlling that and trying to change them is one of the best things to do. You want to be in control of the habit, you don't' want the habit to be in control of you. It's time to take your life back, and it all starts with this.

So what are you waiting for? It's time to start!

I hope you enjoy this book and I hope it gives you a better insight on habits and how they are formed.

1

WHAT IS A HABIT?

This is the first question to tackle; what is a habit? You want to get this out of the way at first so that you can focus on the bigger issue. But for those who don't know that they're perpetuating a habit, this is the chapter that lays it all out for you. This will tell you exactly what a habit is and go into details about the different types of habits that are out there. This will give you firm footing on what to do next, and in the ensuing chapters you'll learn even more about habits and the different nuances of them.

The first thing to talk about is the definition of a habit. A habit, by definition, is a type of thing that you do that is done in a regular manner. It's not something done once in a while; it's something that is done when the right situation is triggered to allow it to come about. For example, if you have something that you need to do, you'll trigger that habit into play. Most habits that you have occur without your knowledge of it. Like if you have a habit of being late, that's something that will happen without your knowledge for the most part. Even if you leave early, you'll probably end up with some sort of traffic getting in the way. It's a pain, but it happens.

A habit is also a fixed way of thinking or acting. Sometimes you naturally have habits that come about, other times you learn them. The ones that occur naturally can be due to environmental factors. For example, if your parents have a habit of being late, you'll end up with a habit of being late.

Some people might notice that they have a habit. If someone has a habit of biting their nails for example, they will have the signs on their fingernails. Other habits aren't all that obvious. If you're late all the time, or if you have a habit of stuttering, you might not even realize it unless people tell you about it. A habit works in mysterious ways, but it's usually something unbeknownst to you and something that you can control.

Sometimes people do notice their habits. One of the ways a person does is they might be able to analyze the way that they're acting. If a person has a habit of being a downer, then the might realize it when they're talking and notice that their entire conversation is all doom and gloom. Some people can see it, but other times they go under the radar. Most people don't' realize them because of the process of how they are formed.

Usually, a person does the habit once, and they don't really take a moment to analyze what they're doing. Instead, they usually just let the habit continue. You continue that habit for as long as you decide to have it around. It can be compulsory, meaning that you do it whether you like it or not. The habit, once it's repeated again and again, starts going onto automatic. That means that it's normally done whether you like it or not. The habit continues to be around because it is imprinted in your neural pathway. Your brain remembers it, and once it does it sends that message once again to various parts of your body. Your body then starts doing that same behavior. It's naturally imprinted, so you won't' have much control over it.

There are also two types of habits that you can have. These are what all habits are divided into. They are called new habits and old habits. They can either be good or bad, but sometimes one is harder to control than the other.

The old habits are ones that you are doing and ones that become ingrained within you over time. They are the ones that you originally have and the ones that are very hard to break. If you start a habit years ago, it can be very hard to get rid of. Old habits are usually the bad ones that you want to get rid of, but have a hard time doing so. If you're able to break it however, you are then successful in getting rid of the bad habit.

Then there is the good habit. These ones are the ones that you decide to create and want to live by. For example, if you decide that you want to start cleaning your room once a week, that's a new habit you're trying to form. Or, if you decide that you want to start making a habit out of bringing your lunch instead of spending money each day at a fast food place, that's another new habit that you can form. New habits are the type that one makes over time. They are valuable if they're good habits, but there is a problem with many habits out there.

The main issue with forming new habits is the idea of forming them. New habits take a lot of effort. You will have to do this consciously until you have the ability to start doing it unconsciously. Once you do it without thinking though, it'll be ingrained. Habit formation can be good, but it takes a lot of work to get it imprinted into your neural pathways.

The way to determine whether or not something is a big habit or a small habit is how much you're able to control it. Some people may have a tiny habit of biting their nails. If it's not repeated though, it starts going away. But, every time a habit is repeated it gets stronger. And when you do the action in the right context, you'll continue to make the habit more powerful. If you don't want a habit to form, don't give into it. Instead, try forming a new one.

The forming of habits can be very slow. Some people can form habits faster than others though. For example, if there is a situation that requires a habit to be formed, it will be done. Some habits take longer to form though. If you've had a habit of binge drinking sodas every day for the last three years of your life, it's going to be harder to kick the habit. It will be very easy to keep the habit around though. Habits take a while to form, but the average time it took for a person to develop one was about 66 days according to a study in 2010. The longest it can be though, can be up to 254 days. That's almost a year of working on a habit!

Habits actually are something that some psychologists have studied. Pavlov, in his study of the dogs and seeing how they acted, worked with examining the stimulus-response mechanism of these creatures. What he did with the dogs is similar to what happens in humans and how a habit is formed. Usually the study of a habit and the process of the formation of a habit can be divided into three parts. They are the cue, the behavior, and the reward. This is similar to how people test on animals. They give them the cue, the person does something, and then they're given the reward. You often see this when you're trying to teach a dog how to sit. They will be given a cue, such as a hand sign, and then they'll do the action. Once they do it right, they'll get the reward. Since humans do have animal like tendencies, the function in this way many times. Humans will want something when they're given the right cue. Once they get the cue, they'll do the action, and then they'll get the reward.

In habit forming, this works the same way. It's shocking, but this is how it's done. A person will get a cue from someone or something that causes the habit to come out. It will trigger the habitual behavior. One can get these triggers from something that your mind associates with as well. For example, if someone sees a soda, they might have a habit of drinking it. They just do it without any reason. This trigger starts the behavior and won't stop it until the action is done. You might not want a soda, but if you have a habit of drinking soda, you'll have one regardless. The action then is the thing that you do with the habit. If you drink a soda whenever you're nervous, you'll get one. You'll probably say that "sodas calm you down" as a justification for this habit. You'll grab one, and then you'll probably drink it without thinking about it. You might not even realize until you finished the soda that you even did it. It's that spooky sometimes. Once you finish it though, it's time for the final thing to happen. That was the reward that you get. When a person tells a dog to sit and they do it on the cue, they usually get a treat. Well, when you're forming a habit, you won't get a treat when you do the action. Least not a physical one. Usually what you'll get is a feeling of relief and a positive feeling. It's kind of like when a person has a caffeine addiction and then drinks a coffee, they'll get the rewarding feeling of feeling better and not as stressed out. When you do that though, you'll soon see that it's the catalyst for something else.

This will then start to continue something called the "habit loop." This is the loop of the same thing over and over again. The cue, the action, and the reward. That's how the person becomes acclimated to doing it. This is how the habits that are usually bad are formed. A person will trigger these habits no matter what. You'll see it in any person, and these habits are hard to quit.

Most of the habits that follow the "habit loop" are those that are hard to quit. They're the ones that are not easy to fix or kick, and soon you'll spiral out of control and unable to do it. Similar to how a person who's addicted to smoking won't be able to go a couple hours without a cigarette, all habits soon get to the point where the person won't be able to control themselves. And at that point, that's when things get ugly.

Habits are pretty crazy, and they can affect a person's life. But they can also help people in a positive way. You can cause the "habit loop" to stop in a negative way. It might be hard, but after a bit you'll soon learn how to change the habit loop so that it's moving in the other direction. You can influence the habit loop so that you can change the way your life is going. All you have to do is follow some of the steps given later on in the book on how to break a habit. Once you start, you'll soon change the way your life is going, and then you'll feel happier as well.

Habits can be a big thing in a person's life, but now that you know what a habit is and how it's formed, you'll be able to have more information on how to beat the habit. If you're still unsure of if your habit is bad or not, the next chapter will talk about the effects of habits and what they can do to your own goals and your future.

2

HABITS AND GOALS

Habits and goals can be linked in certain ways. Have you ever had a goal to lose a certain amount of weight, but you're unable to do something about it even with trying? Well a habit can come into play and it can really affect your achievement of goals. They can also help in a positive manner as well though. In this chapter, we'll explore the pros and cons of a habit in relation to your own goals and what a habit can do when it comes to allowing you to achieve your goals.

The first thing we should talk about is the benefits of having a habit when you're trying to achieve your goals. There are benefits of habits when you're trying to get something. Some habits that you develop over time are helpful to your success. You might have a habit of not procrastinating. It is a habit, and some people are lucky enough to have it. This will affect your overall success because if you do have a habit of that, you'll be able to do things without having to worry about procrastinating. You'll get your assignments done on time, and most of the time you'll even do it before the deadline. That's a good habit to have. If you have a habit that works in the situation that you're in, it'll help you achieve your goals.

But then there's the other issue, the other side of the coin that isn't fun to deal with. That's the idea of the habit affecting your behavior and your ability to do things in a negative manner. A habit can actually cause you to miss out on your goals. You might have a goal to do something, but due to the habit coming into play, you won't' be able to change it. Habits are something that we all can change, but it can affect your overall goals if it's still around. When you have a habit that is negative, the best thing to do is to get rid of it.

Habits and goals are usually learned and memorized. That means that the habits are part of your memory. You'll remember these habits more than you'll remember other things, so you'll have them come into play faster than rational thought at times. The problem with that and goals is if you have a habit and you try to change it, the process can be slow. You might not be able to change the habit in one go. You might need to continue to do that habit for a while before it changes itself. It's a long and arduous process, and if you're trying to change something huge then it's going to take longer than before.

Goals however, can change habits in ways as well. If you have a bad habit, but you want to achieve a goal that's the opposite of the bad habit that you have, you'll feel driven to change it. When you do go for the goal despite the habit though, you're going to feel the pressure of the habit trying to change you. Habits also can cause goals to change by repetition. Habits are a trace of some goal pursuit, and if you have an action that's continued, you'll start moving in that direction.

When you do have the contest between the habit that you have and the goal in mind, there can be an opposition. The opposition is usually a mental thing, but it can cause a lot of problems. The oppositional behavior can really affect you, and sometimes the habit will prevail over the goal. When that happens, your mind will think that the habit is better and use that to its advantage. It can be a vicious problem, and usually it's not something that a person wants. When working on changing a habit, watch out for that. A habit can be used to your benefit, or your downfall when it comes to goals and achieving them.

You can even change your behavior patterns with habits. If you have a behavior that you use when it comes to reaching goals, you could change it by forming a new habit. Let's say you're lazy and unsure of if you're able to actually complete a goal. Well, if you want to change the behavior pattern, you can start implementing a new habit. You can change the way you act by forming a new habit, and you'll be able to place habits into your repertoire that help you to your advantage. It's important to pick habits that will help you instead of harm you. If you pick up a good habit and start to implement it, it can change the automatic processes of the mind. But, in order to actually have habits change you must have a goal. So first pick out what you want your goal to be and change your habits accordingly. By doing that, you'll change the automatic processes of the mind and influences the habits that you already have. Once you do that, you'll start to realize that changing and forming new habits can be easy. All you have to do is try out new behaviors and continue to implement them.

Habits and goals are intimately connected. A habit is the human behavior that you exhibit, and your goal is your aspiration and desire. You'll be able to have a ton of fun and you'll even reach your goals if you have a better control of your habits and you know how to handle them.

3

HOW TO BREAK BAD HABITS

Now that you know how intimately habits and goals are, it's time to look at some of the bad habits that you have. You might be a nail biter, or you might have a habit of smoking. Those habits are both annoying to many people and yourself, but in some cases they can also be a health and life risk as well. You won't be as active in doing what you want to do, and instead you'll be stuck with these bad habits. There is a lot that you can do, but in this you'll find out how to get rid of habits. This section is divided into three parts: how to kick the bad habits that you've been doing for a while, how to get rid of lifelong habits that are so ingrained into you that you can't do a thing about them (or so it seems,) and how to treat short-term bad habits that come into play and are plaguing your life. This is how you treat them, and in this chapter we'll go into detail on why it is you might be doing that habit and how to break it.

The Long-Term Bad habits

These are the ones that many people consider vices. Ones such as smoking, drinking, or even a habit of taking drugs. You might be one of those people that has one of these, but you also might have the habit of being a compulsive shopper, or even sometimes it can be a long-term bad habit of being a compulsive liar. These things can really be a problem in many people's lives, and many say that these long-term bad habits are the reason they're not making their dreams come true. The truth of the matter is, these things are part of the reason why you're not able to make your dreams come true. It's an issue that everyone seems to face, and you might have a vice that needs to be kicked as well. In this section, you'll find out how to get rid of the bad habit.

The first thing is to recognize it. Realize that you have the habit. Some people might use the excuse of smoking so they can relieve stress, or they might drink because they just got out of a bad relationship. These reasons are the reasons for your doing of these actions, but you have to realize that it's a habit. You have to realize that you're the one who put the habit into place. There wasn't' some mysterious force that's compelling you to do it. You trained your brain to imprint the habit into your nerves. You did that, because you decided that it was okay to have that. That's the truth of it, and for many they can't handle it. But you have to first realize that you have a habit before you can break it. Remember, with many things, knowing is half the battle and it's something that you need to recognize first before moving onto the next step.

When you are learning about yourself and realizing you have a bad habit, you should recognize what it's done to you. Most of the bad habits out there have a negative impact on your life. Smoking causes you to stink, have a wheezing cough, and it can stop you from even working out. There is also the factor that you're not able to be as active as you were before. Also remember, smoking costs money, and that's where it burns a hole in your pocket. You may want to look at your financial records as well. Most cartons of cigarettes cost about 40-60 dollars, sometimes a bit cheaper in rare causes. You might go through a carton a week, and it can add up to almost 200 dollars minimally a week if you smoke like crazy. That's a lot of money, and over the years you're wasting thousands of dollars on this thing.

With drinking, it's in the same vein. You might get bottles of wine that cost about 20 bucks. If you go through a bottle a week, that's almost 100 bucks. If you drink beer, usually a pack of that costs around ten dollars. It all adds up, and sometimes it's best to look at the financial state of affairs to see just how bad the habit is.

Also, look at yourself. The only way to break some habits is to take responsibility for it. You have to realize in yourself that you're the cause of your problems. Not the guy down the street, you. Look at what's going on and see how you can take responsibility for it. Even if it's starting off small such as limiting yourself to only one glass of wine a week, or only having one pack a week, it starts to become easier. You want to realize how you can be in control of this and how you can try to change the way things are going. If you do that, and if you monitor how you're taking responsibility for things, you'll soon realize that actually working on this is not as bad as you think.

When you look at yourself, also see how this habit is affecting your goals and why you do it. Some people do things because they're bored, and some do it because they feel like they need to. You should look into yourself and see what is the reasoning for you to do that sort of thing. By looking at that, you'll be able to see for yourself just what it can do to your life if you don't nip it in the bud. Maybe you've always wanted to do one thing but weren't able to because of the habit. That might give you incentive to start getting rid of it. If you look at the way your life is being affected by the habit, you can see for yourself just what it can do to you.

Once you've done that, it's time to start changing the habit. Now, with many habits that are bad for you and have been around for a long time, it's important to realize one thing. You can't get rid of it altogether. At least not right away. Bad habits are so hard to get rid of in many people that you need to realize that it's hard to just quit something and expect yourself to just move on. In some cases, people might be able to do that, but it's not going to be that easy. When you do start to get rid of a bad habit, you want to replace it with something else. You don't get rid of a bad habit, you replace it with something else.

You might replace smoking with chewing gum. If you get the sugar-free gum, you can also help with your health as well. Plus, it keeps your mouth moving, and that can burn calories. If you have the bad habit of drinking sodas, replace it with tea. Same if you're a caffeine addict, replace it with tea. You can start with caffeinated tea, which is actually better for you than coffee, but then once you're off the coffee and such, you can then change it to green tea. Tea is much healthier than soda because of the contents in it. There isn't a ton of sugar like in sodas, and you'll feel better as well. Tea has health properties, and it'll make you feel better when you need something to pick you up.

Other ways to replace it is to play with small toys, or eat something that's healthy. Sometimes, eating carrots instead of smoking cigarettes can help out a lot. Plus, the vitamins in it are beneficial as well. If you have the habit of eating sweets, replace them with fruit. The natural sugars are necessary for the body, and you won't have the crash like with processed sugars. Replacing it is the way to go.

Now, you might now of the perfect way to replace it, but you have no idea how. To do that, you should first decide which day you're going to replace the habits. You might have to start off slow and take a tiny bit of the habit. But, if you can resist it, it's even better. Just say you're not going to do it that day. And then follow through with it. If you see the triggers come about, actually resist them. If someone offers you a cigarette, don't take it. If someone says they want to go to the bar, tell them you would rather not. If they're your friends, they will understand and they will respect you for it.

Then, just continue to chip away at it. The first week is the worst. You'll miss the habit, but replace it with a good one. Don't think you're losing out on things just because you're changing your habits. It's best if you try to fix it up, and remember that once you get rid of the bad habit you can replace it with something better. Not all hope is lost when you kick a habit, you are actually getting something out of it.

And when you're working on it, consolidate the gains. Realize that you're doing something amazing. Write it in a journal, tell your friends and family, heck you can even write about it on social media. What you're doing is a great thing, and it'll inspire others. People will be happy if they want to see you do well, and if you're kicking a habit that you don't' need to have around, you'll be happier in the long run as well

That's how you get rid of the bad habits. Once you start, you'll be able to continue to have success with it.

How to Fix Lifelong Habits

Now, with lifelong habits, you'll have a harder time. These are the ones that have been around all your life. Let's say you maybe have the habit of biting your nails, or even the habit of picking your nose or stuttering. Those things are problems that you've had for the longest time, but due to the fact that you don't know how to eliminate it, they set you back. You might think that it's impossible to get rid of it, but not all hope is lost. In this section, you'll find out how to get rid of bad habits that have been around forever. It is possible, you just need to follow these steps in order to ensure your success.

The first thing is to recognize that you do it. This is similar to the bad habit, but you want to look at the wider range of the effects of it. Think of how this habit has effect you. Have you missed out on opportunities and friendships because of it? Have you disgusted people or caused others to tease you because of it? Has it affected important relationships that you don't want to have affected? These things are questions that you ask yourself. You might have some major setbacks because of the habits, and it's important to think about them. You want to change them, but you don't know how. Well, you have to first think of just what this habit has done to you and how you can fix it. You want to see what the problems of it have been and how it's created issues for you. By looking at the wider range, you can also see the magnitude of the habit and why it needs to be nipped in the bud. It might be hard to face at first, but you'll get over it and soon you'll be able to face the habit with no problem.

The second thing is then see how much you do it and what are the triggers of it. If you stutter when you're nervous, realize that nervous situations put you into that position. If you have a problem with being angry all the time, realize what the triggers are that get you angry. You need to look out for the signs of what causes these types of triggers.

When they are found, think of ways to avoid them. If someone gets you angry, then don't hang out with them. If you get nervous around certain people, take a second to breathe when you talk to them. Don't think that it's okay to just sit around and think that it's unavoidable. The truth of the matter is, it's not avoidable. There are always going to be triggers around and you have to remember that. You will want to think of how to handle the trigger and not become affected by it. It's as simple as that, but it's the best way to get rid of the bad habit you've had for a while.

Now that you've mentally prepared yourself, go out into the world and determine that you will go one day without doing a particular bad habit. Whatever it may be, just tell yourself that you won't do it. You will realize it's going to be hard and you'll probably have issues for a while, but just keep pushing yourself. You can also get help from others too if you feel like you need some assistance on keeping yourself going. If you do that, then you'll realize that you can go a day without it. The first day is the hardest, and you want to make sure that you stick to it. If you need to, get a support group of friends that will help you. They'll make the journey easier on you, and you won't have to worry about things going haywire.

If you start cutting back on the habit, you'll be able to break it. Remember, it is a slow process, but you'll be able to kick it in no time. Just keep yourself going strong, and soon you'll be able to get rid of even the worst of bad habits. And once you do, you'll have a more fulfilling life.

How to Kick Short-Term Habits

There are some bad habits that come around for only a short term. These are the ones that have only happened for a short period of time, but they are cumbersome enough to become a problem for many. You will want to kick this bad habit before it gets worse. This is the window of opportunity that you need to look at and it's the time where you can change the habit before it gets worse. If you have a bad habit, it's important to realize it at this stage and do something about it for the better.

The first thing to do is realize again that you have a bad habit. This might take a bit of time, but if you start to see yourself slipping because of a bad habit you should look into changing it. For example, many people have the bad habit of staying up all night watching TV or playing video games. Let's say you've started doing that and it's affected your life. What you should do is you should look into the fact that you've started this habit and see what it's done. Look at all the times you've slipped up because of this bad habit and then work to see how you can change it. You'll want to do it when you start to notice things going sour though. If you wait for too long, it'll become a long-term bad habit. When it gets to that point, it's a lot harder to quit. So take a look at what it's doing to your life and see how you can change it in order to make things better.

The next thing to do is to look at how long this habit has been around. Look at the triggers that came about because of the bad habit. Look at what has happened to you and what caused you to even take up the habit. When you see those, also look for what happened before that stressed you out so much that you had to take on the bad habit. By doing that, you'll realize that you did have a reason for doing that. There was a trigger that started all of this.

The next step is to not let that trigger affect you. Think of ways to help yourself so you don't' succumb to that bad habit. If you have a bad habit of watching too much TV because you get bored when you go home, think of ways to alleviate the boredom. Read a book or work on a project.

There are hobbies out there which are healthier for a person and can help a person as well. Replace your bad habit with a good habit, and you'll be able to prevent the triggers that cause you to take up a bad habit.

When you finish with that, there is another way for you to kick the bad habit. That is by putting a rubber band on your wrist. Make sure that it's a tight one and one that will fit snug around your hand. When you see the trigger for the bad habit and you give into it, actually snap the rubber band on your hands. Do it hard enough to make it hurt. Yes, this will sting and if you're not the type to condone this type of therapy then don't do it. But, it's a surefire way to get you to stop doing something. When you use the rubber band to hurt yourself because of a bad habit, your brain will realize that doing that means something bad is going to happen. It's kind of like a stimulus-response mechanism that people have. If you get pain from the action, you'll avoid it. It's the same principle in the habit and breaking it. If you realize that a habit is bad, you're not going to do it. That's something important to realize. You want to see that a bad habit can cause some serious issues to you, and you also want to realize that a bad habit can be stopped in this manner. Some might not condone it because of personal reasons, but it is a way to get rid of a bad habit in the short-term.

You can try to quit the habit cold turkey, but that's hard. For a short-term habit, you're still confused and your brain might think it's a good yet bad idea. You're still conflicted, and many times if there isn't anything to replace it with, you'll end up giving in to the habit. So put something there to replace it with and do that instead of just forsaking it altogether. If you do that, you'll be able to kick the habit and get rid of it before it gets worse.

By changing the habits that you have in your life, you'll

be able to live a better and happier life because of it. Habits can be a good thing, but they can also end up being a bad thing too. Bad habits should always be replaced with good habits, for the good habits will sink in. It's going to take time, and you will soon realize it when you're trying to put a good habit into play. But don't' despair. Instead, take the wins as wins and don't be upset when you do fall back and mess up. Just learn from it and move on, and after a while you are going to be able to kick the bad habit for good. It is possible, and with these steps you can get rid of the bad and replace it with the good.

4

HABIT FORMING 101

Now that you know how to get rid of a bad habit, it's time to talk about the lighter aspects. That's the forming of the good habits in order to get rid of the bad ones, or just forming good habits because it's something that you should do. There are thousands of good habits out there. The thing is, society tends to only focus on the bad and not the good. You need to also realize that there are a ton of great habits out there to be formed. The thing is, most people don't' realize it until it's too late. Well, you can form the good habits, and in this chapter we'll talk about to put in the good habits and how to get rid of the bad habits faster.

Time is of the essence to many people. They assume that they need to get rid of a habit as soon as possible. Heck, most people think they should've gotten rid of the habit yesterday. You then ask them why they haven't' and they proceed to think of a bazillion excuses as to why they are not able to kick that habit right away. It's the sad truth of many people. They all think they should get rid of it as quick as they can, but they don't' know how to. They think that it's as simple as saying a couple of magic words and then the habit goes away. No, with habit it takes time and the length of habit forming depends on many factors. There are things one needs to take into consideration before they think getting rid of a habit is that simple.

First and foremost is to realize that you can't' get rid of a habit immediately. It doesn't work that way. The habit is imprinted into the nerves, and your nerves remember this type of thing. Most habits are on automatic response, and you will realize that when you are trying to kick it. It might be normal for you to just pick up a cigarette and start smoking it without even thinking about it. That's the nature of a habit, and most of them are run on automatic. So it's not something you can just get rid of and then call it a day. These things take time, and they do take work. When you start working on it, you'll see just how much work it takes.

When it comes to how much time it takes to get rid of a habit, the average is about three months. Some may say that it takes 21 days. In some cases, that can happen. But most of the time it's not going to take that amount of time. The main reason for this, is because with human experience, you'll start realizing that emotions come into play. Some habits cause negative emotions to come out of you. If you have an addiction to alcohol and have made it a habit to drink three glasses a day, you're probably going to end up having a harder time trying to get rid of a bad habit. Plus, the neuropeptides of the body all have an emotional state and outcome that reinforces them. If you feel happy when you smoke a cigarette, you're going to feel happy when you smoke one. Emotions take a big chunk of the time when you're trying to get rid of a habit, for if you're trying to get rid of something it'll cause them to come into play.

Then there's the fact that some of these habits have

withdrawal symptoms. Smokers that are trying to kick the habit can become some of the most emotional people you've ever seen. They have a wide range of emotions, mainly because they want a cigarette and can't have one. They're trying to reach a goal, but that addiction is gnawing away at them like a puppy with a chew bone. You have to remember that emotions and emotional receptors play a big part in this. They can cause a person to go from happy to sad, and in many cases, it can cause the person to turn uglier than you've ever imagined.

So when it comes to kicking a habit, it depends on the emotions that are brought up. But it also depends on the triggers. If you're in a place with a ton of triggers that set off the emotion, it's going to take you longer. If you're in a place that rarely triggers the action, it'll be easier. You need to look at the triggers as well and try to see how you can influence them. If you surround yourself with people who don't partake in the habit as well, you'll be able to kick it even faster.

You also have to remember the severity of the habit comes into play as well. Short-term habits will go away a lot faster than long-term ones. If you partake in the habit frequently, it's going to take a lot longer to get rid of it. It's just a fact of life. You can't get rid of a bad habit that's been around for so long without the struggle coming into play. You're have the contest between yourself and the goal that you have, and you'll feel the struggle. The struggle can be one of the hardest things about this, and if the habit is very severe, it's going to take longer than three weeks. It can take up to a year in some cases.

With the length of time, the factors are all there. It will probably take about three months, but you need to realize that it could take longer or shorter. It really all depends on what the situation is. Some habits are easier to kick than others, so it's important to realize that before you start kicking yourself and thinking that it's going to be like this forever. You have to work at it, and once you work hard you'll be able to reap the reward without any troubles.

The next thing to think about is how to get rid of a bad habit faster. There are ways to speed this up, and you just have to think of the different ways you can implement this into your life. There is a lot that you can do, but you need to think about how you can influence the way things are and make them even better. You can kick habits faster, and you don't need to suffer as much when you do so.

The first thing you need to do is to make a lifestyle change. That's probably the hardest part for many people, because it might mean that you are going to not hang out with people as much. Or you might not be able to partake in something as much as others can because you're trying to kick the habit. You have to change your life though, for if you get rid of the triggers, it'll make it even easier. You can get rid of the harmful effects of the triggers in your life, and once you do you'll be able to fix up the habit and replace it with a good one. A sacrifice like that is worth it in the end.

Some of the lifestyle changes you might need to make is you might have to avoid friends for a while who do the bad habit. If they're smokers, don't go and hang out with them when they smoke. If you do that, you will be tempted to have a cigarette. If some people exhibit the bad habit that you're trying to quit, you'll realize soon enough that you won't be able to do it if you're getting tempted all the time. You should decide to hang out in places where the habit isn't done a whole lot. Don't' go to bars if you're trying to not drink as much or kicking the habit of drinking. If you love sweets, don't go to a candy store. Just stay in places where you won't' get tempted. Also, you should tell your friends about the habit and the fact that you're kicking it. If they're your real friends, they will understand and try to make things comfortable for you. If you do that, you'll be even less tempted to do things like that. You'll be willing to change your lifestyle and all of the choices that you've made in order to help change your life for the better. It's good to do, and once you start you'll be able to have a better time as well.

If someone does offer you a thing you're trying to quit, don't' get mad at them. Some people are uninformed and they might think it's okay to give you that stuff. Just politely decline and tell them you're trying to break the habit and don't want to start it up again. People will be happy if you do that, and it'll be better for you as well.

If you want to break it faster, you should set up the area that you live in and your lifestyle choices so that you don't get tempted. If the temptation isn't' there, you won't' want to give into it. It's as simple as that, and if you keep at it, it'll go faster. The only way you can slow down kicking a bad habit is if you give into it and think you should do it for some reason. You don't need a bad habit to make life better, and once you kick it you'll be able to have a better life than you've ever imagined for yourself. You deserve to be happy, and you'll soon see that you can create your own happiness just by changing your lifestyle.

When it comes to putting good habits in faster, this can be hard for many. Good habits are hard to learn and take a while to implement. The problem is, it's something new so your body won't be familiar with it. Your body knows what good and bad habits are for you and the body also knows what will help you and what won't. Right now, the body thinks that having the bad habit will help you do better, when in reality it'll only hurt you and create issues for you in the end. The body also thinks that having a good habit is going to take forever to learn. Since it's different from the bad habit, the body might try to reject it and give into the temptation of the bad habit. You don't need to do that though. There are ways to kick the bad habit and ways to allow you to be happier as well.

When it comes to good habits, work to put them in. Good habits just don't' magically fall into place, they require blood, sweat, and tears for them to really sink in. It's important to realize that bad habits are formed very fast and good habits are hard to put in. That's because you're trying to change a grooved in idea. But, if you continue to work at it, you will chip away the bad and replace it with the good. It will take energy, but the struggle is real and worth it.

When it comes to putting in a good habit, take it one step at a time. Don't start thinking six months into the future just yet. Let time continue to flow and continue to keep on trucking. Don't think that everything will change for the better with just one tip. Life doesn't work that way. Instead, take each day as one step, and soon you'll be happier as time goes on.

A final thing to think about when forming good habits is to reward yourself when you do something right. This doesn't mean take up the bad habit for a moment. No, that will only set you back. Taking up a bad habit for a moment as a reward is a foolish thing to do. For one, it confuses the body and the body will assume that it's okay to do that again. The body will think that just because you did it once, you'll have free reign to act that way once again. That's not the case. That's not a reward as well. It's more of a punishment for doing good, and your body might think that getting rid of the habit is a bad thing. Your brain needs to realize that you are the one in control. It needs to realize that you're the one creating this whole situation and you're the one who wants to change it. So, instead of trying to reward yourself with a small taste of the bad habit, think of a better reward. Maybe you can buy a little something for chipping away at a bad habit. That small reward adds up over time, and you'll feel happy for changing your life. You need to realize that it's something you're going to have to work at, and if the reward is fitting, it'll be worth the time and effort.

Kicking a bad habit can be a nightmare in some people's heads. The idea of getting rid of something you're so indoctrinated in might be unpalatable to some. But, if you get rid of the bad and replace it with the good, you'll soon realize that life is better that way. And you'll be able to reach your goals, which is something more important than a little habit. Good habits cause better goals to come about, and you'll be happier as well.

5

EFFECTIVE TIME MANAGEMENT

When it comes to habits, one of the worst that people have is managing time. There are so many distractions out there that people give into them like no other. They think that these distractions are good for them, but they actually make things a whole lot worse. There is a way to beat this though, and in this chapter you'll find out how to beat the clock and have a better time with having effective time management.

The first thing you need to do when it comes to managing time is to look at yourself. Look at what you're trying to get done. Look at the goals that you have and aspirations that you have. Look at how you can use your time in order to make things better. If you look at yourself and see that you need a certain amount of time in order to make sure that you get things done, you'll see that you need to have that time in order to achieve your goals. Looking at the broad picture can help.

The next thing, once you've looked at the broad picture, is to make a plan. A plan for this is the overall goal that you have and how in the world you're going to get to it. Some goals are huge, such as trying to run the marathon or getting to a goal weight, but you can achieve them. You should look at everything that you need to do in order to achieve the goal that you have. It's not something that will take five minutes to do, but if you have a plan it'll make things easier. You want to have an exact set of steps that you'll need to do in order to get to the state that you want to be in. If you want to run the marathon, plan out how you're going to run it. Go through the exact steps, and you'll soon see the overall things that you need to do in order to get to that point. It might look daunting at the moment, but if you work at this, you'll see that the dreams that you have can become a reality if you follow the overall game plan that can help with your goals.

The next thing is to make a monthly plan. You look at exactly what you want to accomplish this month. It can be goals that are big or small, but don't bite off more than you can chew. Thing about what you can realistically do in order to hit a certain goal. You have to look at what you need to change in order to accomplish all of those things. A monthly plan allows you to change the way things go, and you can also change the way life goes as time passes. A monthly plan will keep you on track and motivated to keep on going with the goals that you have in mind.

Next, think of how the goal can be divided into four weeks. Dividing it down and making sure that you have a good plan in order to get to the goal by the date makes it easy. At first, it may look like hell on earth to you. You might think the idea of actually going through with this to be something on the order of trying to beat a god or something. But, in reality you need to see that if you divide it up in a logical way that it is doable. Any goal that you have is completely doable. You need to just put it in a plan of action and stick to it. By doing it in a daily way, you can chip at it in order to make the huge goal something that you can face.

When you make the daily plan, allow yourself time to put in that goal every day. Going a day without the goal in mind can make things hard on you. You need to leave it there for you to see. If you need to, write it on a sickly note and put it on your fridge. Every single day you'll see that you can reach the goal, and you'll feel motivated to actually work on it and not let it fall by the wayside. You want to have a strong life full of things to do, and putting the goal there each day will get you ready for you to face the hardship of the giant goal.

When you have it all planned out, it's time to actually do it. Even if you think it's one of the worst days ever, you want to have the goal there and work on it. You'll want to dedicate the amount of time that you need to in order to make sure that you reach the goal. It doesn't have to be a lot, but if you make a plan you'll be able to get everything that you need to done. You won't have it hanging around in your head for a long time. You'll also stay on top of things and not let the issues of your laziness take over.

Another thing that you should do is you should always get it done first. It doesn't matter if you need to wake up a tiny bit earlier just to get everything that you need to done for it. Doing it first thing will make things that much better on you. And, if you work on the goal at first, you'll be pumped for the rest of the day. Being pumped and inspired to continue will allow you to continue to make sure that your goals are reached and you're happy.

By doing it first thing and achieving it each day, it also causes morale to be raised. When people are lazy, most of the time they feel like crap. That might be because they don't like just sitting around, but there are other things involved with it as well. You can let you remind wander into places it doesn't need to go when you're sitting around and being idle. It could cause you to think all sorts of weird things, and that's just putting it mildly. By actually making sure that you stay focused, you'll feel better and get more done.

You should also keep yourself motivated. Some days are just draggy and most people hate them. The dog days do happen, and most people hate them. It can be a big issue for so many people, since dog days usually cause people to not want to do anything despite trying. But don't let them get to you. Even if you feel like complete dirt and you just want to sit around and binge-watch Netflix, don't. Don't' do that. Laziness is like a sickness, and if you let that habit in, it'll open up the door for laziness to continue. Instead, keep working on your goals, but also have a plan for what you want to do every single day. Just make up a list of everything that you want to get done, and then just do it. It doesn't take a ton of effort to do so, you just need to have the drive and desire to continue on. It can suck for a while, especially if you're the type who is used to being lax and not doing anything. But, if you knock off the laziness for at least one day, you'll soon realize that at the end of the day, you actually accomplished more than most people. The feeling of accomplishment is remarkable, especially when you accomplish many things. If you keep yourself motivated and want to continue to work, you'll realize later on that doing that could be one of the best things you've ever done for yourself.

Another thing to do in order to help keep time better managed is to get rid of distractions. This one is probably the hardest thing for most people. It's not even the cell phone or the computer. It can be the animals that are making noise, the sound of other appliances, and even the dialogue of people. Distractions are rampant in things, and if they're not taken care of in an effective manner, they can cause a person to easily get sidetracked. Humans are fallible in the fact that they get super sidetracked and off their course easily. One little thing can usually send most people into a tizzy all day. One bad message, or even a good one from a friend, can distract you for god knows how long. You need to realize that these distractions, although nice to have every once in a while, should be eliminated from your life. When people want to talk, just tell them that you're working on something. Some might get offended, but you have to remember that this is your life. You need to make sure that you're getting everything that you need to get done accomplished. It's not that hard, and you have to remember to just keep on going and not care what people think. You're trying to reach your goals, and if a person gets joy out of distracting you from reaching your goal, then they don't deserve to be a friend to you right now. You want to surround yourself with people who support you, and if you need to eliminate them for a bit so you don't' get distracted, it will help you out even more so later on.

A final thing is to reward yourself when you use time effectively. If you get everything that you needed to get done accomplished that day, then that's grounds to celebrate. It's not hard to do, and when you realize it you'll see you've accomplished a big feat. Don't get yourself anything too extravagant until you reach your final goal. Instead, reward yourself a little bit each day whenever you get everything that you need to get done accomplished. You will be happier, and you'll be able to use time to become more efficient as well.

Time efficiency is something everyone struggles with. Everyone seems to have the problem of staying on track and using time wisely. It might be a problem for you, but this chapter laid it all out and proved to you that you can use time in a wise and efficient manner. You will be happier, and you'll also reach your goals, which is something that feels amazing.

6

TIPS TO HELP COPE WITH BAD HABITS

Bad habits are great to get rid of, and if you're able to nip them in the bud, there's more power to you. It's amazing when you finally take that step and start trying to alleviate a bad habit. There is one problem with it though: that is the fact that you're going to run into a slew of problems when you start trying to get rid of it. Bad habits come with their own set of emotions that are a pain to deal with sometimes. They might get so strong that people might think it's best to avoid you, which isn't always the case. A bad habit can put a ton of stress on yourself, but you can cope with it in order to get rid of it. In this chapter, the discussion of how to cope with bad habits comes into play. You'll find out the best ways to get rid of the stressful elements of bad habits as well, and that will help you feel better when you're trying to change the bad habit that you have.

The first thing is to breathe. Bad habits take a lot out of you, and you need to just take a moment and step back. Take a second to breathe and just not think about it. Don't think about anything for the matter, for it might cause you to think about the stress that you're dealing with. Take a moment to just think about nothing and take a moment to de-stress. Breathing will calm you down and allow you to think clearly. Sometimes you just need to take a second to chill out, and you'll be able to feel better and be happier as well.

The next thing is to get rid of the stressful elements when you're trying to quit a habit. If you're around people who cause nothing but stress for you, don't' associate with them. You don't' need that negativity in your life, and if you just get rid of that, you'll feel calmer. Some people don't' like it when others do well and try to get rid of their bad habits. Those people will only cause you to want to partake in the habit even more. When that happens, just get them out of your life. You can do it as a temporary thing, but if they're going to be mean about it, you don't need to have that in your life. Think about the types of people you want to hang out with, and you'll soon realize that there are some people that you would just not associate with.

Another thing to help get rid of the stress is to not be in stressful environments. Some people might feel the habit start to get triggered when they're in certain areas. Obviously you can't stop going to work just because it stresses you and the habit out, but you can get rid of places that might tempt you. If some people in the office smoke, don't go out with them when they take their smoke breaks. If you see that some of your friends want to go out and have sweets, even though you're trying to kick the habit of eating too much, politely decline or try to see if there's a better place you can go to that's not going to tempt you. The environments of certain places are prone to affect a person in ways they might not like. When you're in places that make you feel like you have to do the bad habit, it will only stress you out and make you feel worse. Get rid of that element in your life, and look for ways to help you de-stress in places that make you feel welcome and accepted.

Also, you should tell people about what you're doing. Some might not realize that you're trying to make a change, and they might think it's okay to take you to all the places that you went to in the past. As flattering as it can be, you don't want to spend your time in those environments. They'll only make you feel worse. Instead, just inform people on your life choices, and they will respect them. If they don't, then were they really your friends? Probably not, and you should look for ways to help make your experiences all the more better.

Another thing that you can do is think happy thoughts when the feeling of the stress starts to kick in when you're dealing with a habit. Think of the good things that will come out of it. Better yet, think of good things that don't' have anything to do with the bad habit. Look at the good side of life, not the bad. You should think about the best things in the world when you feel the urge and stress of the situation start to come over you. Just take your time, and you'll feel better as well. You want to think happy thoughts when you're going through this, for if you don't, then you're only going to feel worse as well.

A great way to help deal with the stress of the habit as well is to take up a hobby. A hobby is a great way to help keep your mind occupied. There are many different hobbies out there, and some are perfect for those who are trying to get away from the habits that they might be tempted to partake in. You can try sewing, crocheting, and even things like fishing and running can help. Plus, you can make things out of it or do something good for yourself when you do these hobbies. Many times habits that you have only cause bad things to happen, but if you take up the hobby and do something with it instead of just trying to think only of the habit, you'll realize you'll have something more fun to deal with in your life. Adding more fun to your life will allow you to think about the other things that you have and not think of the habit.

With hobbies, you can also meet new people. You can tell them about yourself and the struggle that you're going through. There are even support groups for some of these habits that are more than willing to help you out. They understand what you've been through and they will help you alleviate the desire and temptation that you might have. They've been there before, and sometimes it's best for people to go to these groups. It's filled with individuals with the same habits, and they might be able to give you some insight on how to help cope with the stress that comes from having these bad habits. It's something that will help you, and if you help yourself then you're going to feel better as well. Meeting people who understand the struggle and just what you're going through can be one of the best things out there, and if you meet someone who knows what the pain of quitting your habit can entail, you'll feel better. Life can be hard, but if you travel it with people who are willing to bring you up and make you feel better, it will make the struggle of quitting the habit worth it.

If you do fall on your face and give into the habit, there is one thing you should do. Don't kick yourself. That's one thing so many people do when they start quitting habits and they mess up. They become stressed out about it because they make themselves feel bad. They think that just because you messed up once, you are the worst person in the world. The truth of the matter is, you're not the worst person and it's not the end of the world if you mess up once or twice. If you're using the system of inflicting pain in order to get yourself to kick the habit, you might feel bad. But you have to remember that you're doing this for something better. You're not just doing this because it is a cool idea, or because you're trying to be different or something. You're doing this for yourself, and you have to remember that you are the one that you're trying to fix. Someone is not going to magically come and save you, you're going to have to work at it. So don't take the losses as something to stress out over, just see them as a mistake and learn from it. Correcting your mistakes and actually doing something about the fumble instead of stressing out over it can help you and make the journey easier.

Another thing to keep in mind as well is to take a step back and chill out when the emotions come about. Emotions are strong when you're trying to kick a habit. You're going to become frustrated, angry, and probably sad with yourself. You're going to feel the pain of the struggle. It is a struggle, and many people don't realize what you're going through. They might never realize the pain of trying to quit a bad habit. But you need to remember when you're stressed out and feeling the emotions start to hit you that you're a strong and beautiful person. You're doing something better than what most people can do, and it's a struggle that's harder than many things out there. Most can't even begin to fathom how to get rid of a bad habit, and the emotions that come about with it can be hard. But there is a way to cope with them. If the emotions become too much for you, you should just go to a space where you can be alone. If you need to let out some of the stress and emotions, do so. Just take a moment to let it out and then chill for a moment. Think about everything that has happened and everything that you've been working for. Sure it can be hell on earth for many people, especially the ones who are not used to being under this much pressure. But it's all for a good cause. It really is. You just need to remember that you're doing something amazing, and these emotions are only temporary. You should just give yourself a pat on the back and move on, for that's the best thing you can do.

When it comes to coping with stress from habits, don't let the small things get to you. There are so many small things that can be triggers to you, and sometimes you might feel the urge to just go crazy. But don't let the small stuff cause you to get frustrated. Worry only about the big goal that you have in mind. Think of the big picture, the goal that you have in mind, and soon it'll all be better. Life will be easier, and if you just give yourself pats on the back and feel good when you do something right, things will get better and you will be happier.

All of these tips are great ways to help cope with stress. It's something that pretty much everyone will deal with when it comes to getting rid of bad habits, but if you just take it slow and don't sweat the small stuff, it'll get easier. It will get easier, you just have to trust yourself and keep at it.

7

TIPS FOR PROCRASTINATION

Probably the other bad habit everyone seems to have in life is procrastination. Some people may think waiting until the last minute is the key to success, but in reality it is the double-edged sword that will kill you if you don't take care of it right. Sometimes you might work better under pressure, but procrastinating until the night before to do something and then staying up all night thinking about it can haunt you. You'll end up feeling worse than you've ever felt before. Procrastination comes to haunt you if you keep it around, and it's one of the worst habits out there. Not only does it affect you, but it also affects your peers as well. People rely on you, and if you're waiting on things until the last minute, you won't be able to be trusted. People will just think you're going to screw things up and keep everyone stressed. Plus, it's unnecessary stress, which is something that people don't need in this day and age. From work projects to school projects, to even just doing daily things, procrastination can affect anyone in all areas.

Procrastination might seem like one of those things that

is unavoidable. After all, since everyone procrastinates, it's okay for you to do it. The thing is, it's not advisable to procrastinate on everything. Procrastinating on things will only cause more trouble than it's worth, and just because you're able to be successful with it once, doesn't mean it's going to work in your favor later on. You'll get addicted to doing things like this, and it will take your laziness to a whole new level until you're able to face it. Which is usually when the deadline is right around the corner. You don't need that stuff in your life, and you can beat procrastination. You just have to follow the steps mentioned here, and you'll be able to get rid of the desire to procrastinate.

The first thing you need to do is to look at the way you act when you procrastinate. Most people think that they work best under pressure, but in reality getting things done actually makes a person feel better. Plus, you'll be able to look over the job and see if there are any mistakes, and you'll be able to polish it. You'll be able to hone your skills and abilities, and instead of turning in something that is made on a rush, you'll be able to turn in something perfect that people will enjoy.

Some people think that procrastination is the best thing ever. They say that it gets you motivated, but in reality it stresses you out and causes you to make hasty decisions without thinking. You'll be putting extra stress on yourself, which isn't bad if it weren't for the fact that you probably have about ten other things to think about. The stress plus the procrastination causes you to switch moods and become emotional over everything. People become crazy when they're under stress, and not in a good way either. Procrastination can also bring out the worst in people, and some might be turned off from talking to you until you're done with screaming to the high heavens at them because you didn't' finish your project on time. Think about the stress that procrastination causes you. If you got it done early, you wouldn't have to worry about spending all that time worrying and you'll be able to spend more time feeling happy and accomplished.

Procrastination can also affect your sleep and nutrition. That's another thing that you have to think about and analyze. Procrastination usually causes people to stay up all night, leaving them dead tired the next day. The tiredness causes them to be less rational and will make them think that illogical things are sensible. They'll think that something they put in the project is correct, when in reality they're dead wrong. It's not something that can help you. Instead, it will drain your energy and cause you to be an energy-starved mess until the project is over. It's the same in the food aspect of things. Food and nutrition is important for you to stay focused. When people procrastinate, they might go almost an entire day without eating anything, and most of the time they're spending their time living off of energy drinks and junk food. That will cause your body to become unhealthy, and the health problems will come to bite you over time. Food and nutrition is something that you need to think about, and if you're having issues with anything regarding nutrition and sleep, you should stop procrastinating before it gets worse.

A final bad thing about procrastinating is that it doesn't always work. Most of the time, the person gets lucky if the boss or teacher likes it, or if they get what they need completed on time. One might think that procrastinating is the way to success, but that's far from the truth. In fact, most of the time procrastinating will make you perform worse, because you're working so fast to get this whole thing done that you need to worry about that instead of making sure that you're at the top of your game. It's a shame, but most people don't realize that and think the lie of "procrastination is the key to success" is a truth. It's not, and you'll only feel miserable in the end if you do that. It might seem like a good idea the first time, but most of the time it stops being as effective once you realize just how different your potential is when you do things early and take your time with it.

Now that you know what can come out of being a procrastinator and just how ugly it can be, it's time to look at the ways to change it. Yes, you can change your procrastination in some simple steps, and you'll soon see that it's not as hard as you may think. Most people think the idea of changing your behavior is the hardest thing in the world to do. In reality, it's not and people need to realize that. You can change the way you act and your habit of procrastination with these simple steps, and you'll see after a while that things are better if you do them when you first get them instead of trying to finish everything at the last minute like most people.

Now, the first thing to do after you recognize the problems of procrastination is to look at how you can stay on top of things. It might be something as small as a little reminder or as big as making a calendar of events. You need to take a look at how you can personally stay on top of your game and make sure you don't miss a thing. It's advisable to get a calendar and start filling it out. People need to look at things over a general period of time. You can't just think only looking at the next day is the best thing. You need to look into the future and plan for the future, for if you don't you'll only create issues later on.

Some might not like the calendar method, and if they don't they can just write down what they need to get done in life. This can be a list of a few things or one with hundreds of things. Look at everything that you need to get done, and then divide it into smaller and smaller increments. This is similar to the way you manage your time, but this is related to just the project or the set of things you need to get done. Just put them all in and set up a list of them. Then, you can check off everything that you do in order to keep on top of your game.

With the calendar method, put the dates down for when things need to be turned in. It might be nice to do just that, but you're going to end up procrastinating if you just leave things at that. That's the lazy way to do things. What you need to do at this point is schedule out each day what you need to get done in order to make that target for the day so that you can reach your goal with ample time to spare. Some days might be easier than others, but if it is easy one day, look over the work that you have done on the action and make sure everything is okay. You want to make sure that everything is in order and monitored each day. You don't want to put everything on one day. That's the way you've been doing it before, and that only leads you down a path you don't' want to take. Instead, stretch it out over a period of time. You'll soon see that it's not as bad as you think it is either.

If you're trying to procrastinate because you think the project is too big, think of the way things will be if you leave it like that for that long. You'll think that it's okay to leave it like that for three weeks because it's a giant project, but it's only going to look bigger as time goes on. Instead of worrying about things like that for an extended period of time, just do it now and chip away at it. You'll have way less of a headache if you do. Plus, if you spread it out over a period of a couple weeks, you'll see that it's not as bad as you think it is. That will allow you to be in control of it and not be affected by it.

Once you have everything laid out, it's time to be motivated about it. The motivation can be as small as feeling happy that you got the thing done, or it can be the happiness of not having to worry about it. You're probably going to have to push yourself at first. Most people who want to stop procrastinating after being a procrastinator for so long have a hard time with this. But, if you just remember that there is something good at the end of it, you'll see that it's worth the fight. You need to have the motivation therefore it'll be the best thing for you to have when it comes to dealing with the stresses of finishing the project.

When the day hits that you have to work on the project, it's the time to get yourself moving on it. It might be hard when you first start, but you need to work on it. You need to stick to the plan and work on the goals. Even if it's hard for you to do that, you'll be able to finish the project in no time. Just keep the motivation there and do it. Don't' let your laziness get the best of you. Set a time for you to do it and then do it.

Another thing that goes along with this is the distractions. That's a big thing with procrastinators. They love to distract people and will make sure that they can be distracted by anything. It doesn't have to be something big; even the tiniest of distractions are a problem for these people. But you don't' have to let them bother you. If you take the distractions and throw them off to the side while you work, you'll be able to get the project done. It might be hard, but if you push at it you'll feel better as well.

All of these ways will help you become better at not

procrastinating. It's something that happens over time, and you'll soon see that you can get rid of procrastination without having to fight too hard for it. Procrastination is one of the worst habits out there, but if you nip it in the bud, it will go away over time, leaving you with a more organized and happy life.

AFTERWORD

Habits are both good and bad. You have to realize that there are good habits to have along with bad ones. The world isn't' just a bad place, it's one filled with good things too. You just have to learn to deal with the habits and get rid of the bad things. You can have a life filled with good habits, and you can get rid of the vices that you have.

Habits can empower you. When you have good habits around and work on the good habits, it will start to show through. Others will notice it, and most people will applaud you for having good habits. You can help others learn better habits and get them to be inspired to have a life full of great habits as well. If you do that, everyone will feel better about themselves, and you'll feel better as well.

I hope this book helped you understand the importance of habits and the fact that they can affect a person in many ways. I hope this book opened your eyes so you can see just what happens if you let a habit come between you and your goal. It might be messy, but at the same time you need to come to terms with yourself and work to make yourself the best person you can be. Habits can help you, and if you have the right ones in your arsenal, you will be happy.

I hope this book helped you understand the power of habits. It's time to go out there and change the bad habits and put in the good ones. I know you can do it.

www.ingramcontent.com/pod-product-compliance
Lightning Source LLC
Chambersburg PA
CBHW052125110526
44592CB00013B/1756